Double-Parked, with *Tosca*

Ellen Kaufman's poems look closely at the diurnal . . . and through image and tone make those seemingly familiar spheres strange and haunting.
— Camille-Yvette Welsch, *Foreword Reviews*

Ellen Kaufman's poems pierce the reader the way a needle pierces fabric. With a stunningly precise apprehension of the real, she stitches immigration histories and the intimacies of family life, cityscapes and suburban developments, the recent past and the perilous future. She has the power to shapeshift, too, so that we experience, as if from inside, the hidden life of a retired battleship, an algae bloom, a bird nesting in a traffic light. Marked by grief, endurance, and the truths of beauty made manifest, these are essential poems.
— Jennifer Barber, author of *Works on Paper; Given Away; Rigging the Wind*; founding editor of *Salamander*

As a young person, the best poem I ever read in my life was a Petrarchan sonnet by Ellen Kaufman—before I even knew what a Petrarchan sonnet was. Now, in reading Ellen Kaufman's newest book, *Double-Parked, with* Tosca, I immediately see everything I want poetry to be: imaginative, evocative, observant, musical, filled with sound and living breath, and brilliant. I can't recommend this book and this author enough.
— Nicholas Samaras, author of *American Psalm, World Psalm; Hands of the Saddlemaker (Yale Series of Younger Poets)*

Kaufman demonstrates a technical mastery that bespeaks
her experience in reviewing poetry, using many traditional forms
and patterns while keeping to mainly contemporary subjects. . . .
Her word choices are unerring and her aim is true. Each poem is
a finely tuned instrument that plays a different chord in the heart.
— André T. Demers, *NewPages*

[Kaufman] make[s] the familiar extraordinary. . . . One of this
poet's gifts is the ability to imbue tasks with emotional resonance.
— Doris Lynch, *Library Journal*

Oh, the rewards of a middle-aged female poet's gimlet eye!
Ellen Kaufman's absolutely terrific second book can fearlessly slash
through pretext, but also cohere unlikely pairs through the X-ray
delicacy of an ace metaphorist. She can use "he wanted to get laid"
as a refrain in a satisfyingly avenging villanelle, and also see how a
beret looks like a "fluffy flounder," and a chandelier handed down
through generations "rattles like a skeleton." A tick can alternate
stanzas with its host, and an orchestra can create a landscape from its
instruments. Kaufman uses form—including a masterful crown of
sonnets about her father's end of life—and the speaker herself takes
form in persona poems of NYC landmarks; of the *USS Intrepid*, she
writes, "the old moon / shuttle Discovery perches / like an aphid
on a rose leaf." I bet you never heard that before! And so you will
feel about this whole body of poems. Kaufman's wit, her craft, her
vision—this book celebrates their collaboration.
— Jessica Greenbaum, author of *Spilled and Gone;
The Two Yvonnes; Inventing Difficulty*

Double-Parked, with *Tosca*

POEMS BY
Ellen Kaufman

ABLE MUSE PRESS

Able Muse Press

Library of Congress Cataloging-in-Publication Data

Names: Kaufman, Ellen (Poet) author.
Title: Double-parked, with Tosca : poems / by Ellen Kaufman.
Description: San Jose, CA : Able Muse Press, 2021.
Identifiers: LCCN 2019059804 (print) | LCCN 2019059805 (ebook) | ISBN 9781773490663 (paperback) | ISBN 9781773490670
Subjects: LCGFT: Poetry.
Classification: LCC PS3611.A8265 D68 2021 (print) | LCC PS3611.A8265 (ebook) | DDC 813/.6--dc23
LC record available at https://lccn.loc.gov/2019059804
LC ebook record available at https://lccn.loc.gov/2019059805

Printed in the United States of America

Cover image: from the series *A Year on Broadway* by Elise Engler
Cover & book design by Alexander Pepple

Able Muse Press is an imprint of *Able Muse: A Review of Poetry, Prose & Art*—at www.ablemuse.com

Able Muse Press
467 Saratoga Avenue #602
San Jose, CA 95129

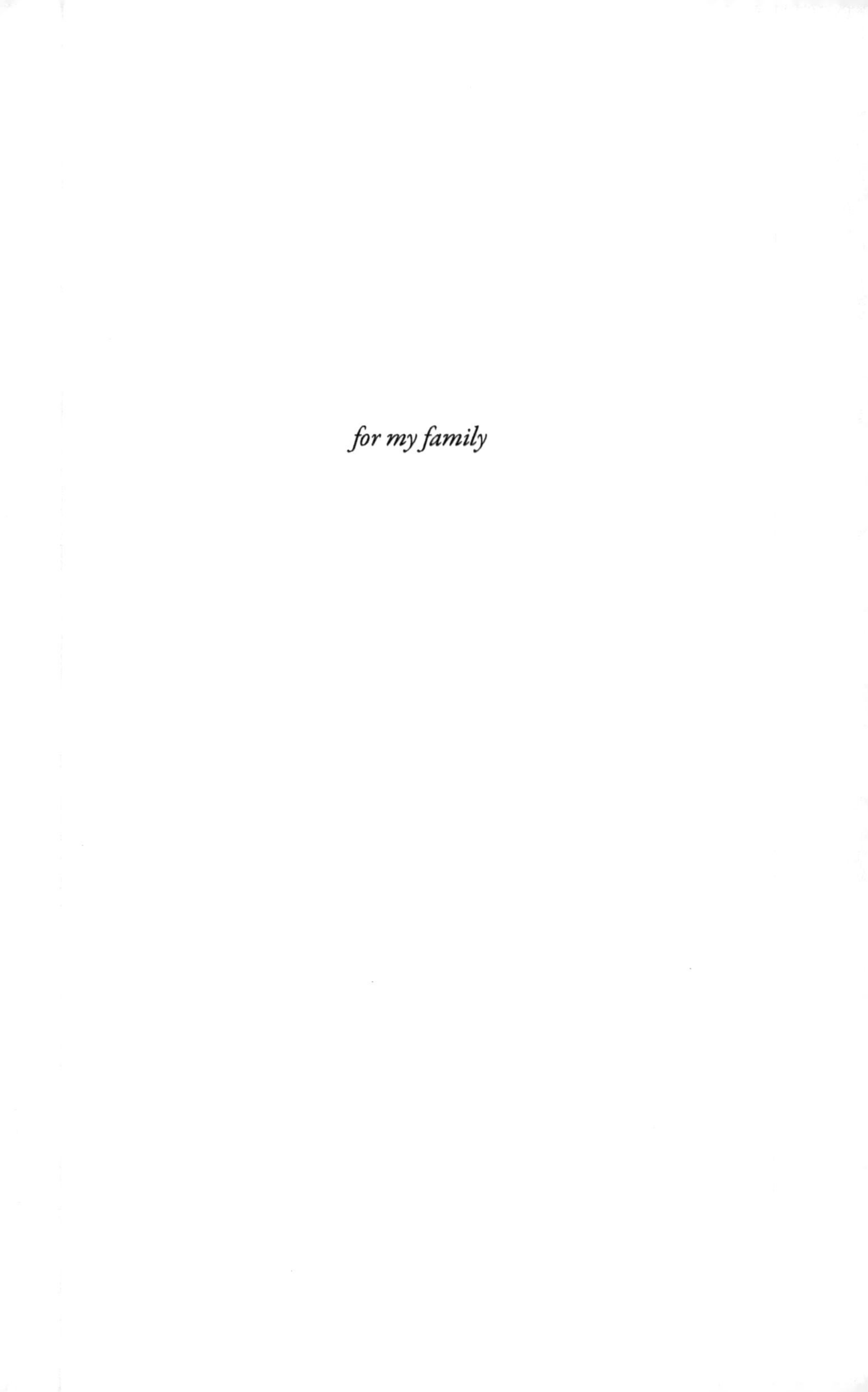

for my family

Acknowledgments

I am grateful to the editors of the following journals, where many of these poems originally appeared, sometimes in earlier versions:

Adirondack Review: "Algae"

Beloit Poetry Journal: "Wire Artist"

Epoch: "Progression"

Hampden Sydney Poetry Review: "Reverse Farm"

Salamander: "Cherries of Kenwood," "The Ice Pond," and "Audiology" excerpt

Tar River Poetry: "Horses"

upstreet: "Fittings" and "Development"

The Yale Review: "Old Dress"

My warmest thanks to the poets who read and responded to this manuscript prior to publication: Jenny Barber, Jess Greenbaum, and Nicholas Samaras.

Thanks also to MacDowell for two residencies in New Hampshire, where some of these poems progressed.

The eponymous *Tosca* was a thrilling 2018 production performed by the Metropolitan Opera and broadcast on WQXR.

Thanks to Michael and Laura Mezey Kaufman, who supplied the genealogical research used in "Terroir."

"Old Dress" samples W. H. Auden's "The Fall of Rome" as well as John Keats's "Endymion."

"Buon Natale" is in memory of Barbara Bloch Larson.

"Reverse Farm" is for Tom Merwin.

Finally, special thanks to Alex Pepple, founder and gifted editor of Able Muse Press, for continuing to support my work.

Contents

Double-Parked, with *Tosca*

Phone Booth

Metal eater.
Chamber pot.
A bellowing

outside my dream.
Today it left
sideways in a bucket

loader, filled with
all the memories.
Where it was is

bandaged up, waiting
for the next idea.
Hold, please.

Strung out or strung
along, people wept
inside it, bled there

into corners.
Call me back, they said,
at this number.

So Many Owls

A sudden influx of awesome
strigidae—
small and large night
types have been spotted
asleep in naked
branches, a curious migration
blind to growing fame.

Some names: saw-whet
(the tiny one) and barred.
A screech was photographed
inside a cherry cloud
of exploded cardinal. And one great
horned was seen

dozing outside the zoo.
A bumper crop
of mice, perhaps, or paucity of prey
elsewhere, some territorial
disruption or dispute
has brought them here
to multiply

on devices
and in the imagination
as they disappear from Earth.
Omens of anything, bright eyes
unlit, parked
on the winter porch
of hawk and falcon:
silently, they gather
disciples.

Old Dress

The look: Elizabethan, with a dropped
hourglass waist, cotton lawn instead
of satin, a tight pleated bodice topped
with tiers of ruffles, and a full skirt wed

to stiffened tulle to give it extra girth.
Budded in blue, the ribbon trim is Keats:
a flowery band to bind us to the earth
at waist and neck and where the ankle meets

the atmosphere above "the perfect shoe."
Fantastic grow the evening gowns: they grew
as empires fell. But now the polar caps
undress themselves, dropping their white lace slips
from virgin spoils of land while our despair
is fashioned into one hot thing to wear.

Estuary Lives

Land under water, land under ice,
land holding bears, panthers, wolves, foxes,
lynx, beaver, rabbits, rattlesnakes, and deer;
the dispossessed and the established,
the native soil, the "foreign elements"
on new slate sidewalks born
from mud and planks.
Wind and fire crossed the uses.
In each ward, the DNA lined up
and waited to be counted,
to braid itself together into bread.
A parallel universe, isthmuses
and peninsulas beyond islands, flat as sea,
held a red-tinged view of the refinery.
Not far from cliffs and waterfalls,
smoothed by the same glacier into
the lowest of plateaus, you could walk
straight into the bay containing Newark,
New York, Delaware, England, Russia.
A concert grand consumed one house,
bumping into singers and players,
the children spilling out and spilling over
into life and death—how did they keep track.
Cows, chickens. A way to slay. The street
car. Crossing water with a linen cart.
Money came later, and it came like rain,
like polio. Like a melted glacier separating

land from land. Each name noted
in spidery cursive on the census list,
handled and microfilmed into yellow
crumbs: Rose, Clarisse, Ethel, Joe, Sara,
Israel, ashes, dust. Thirteen children.
Check the stones. Check the records
as they turn electric, into light and heat.
Rioting workers on the street, a mob
from the refinery, the working poor.
Teachers and learners. Give me your
tired, your War. Two wed and crossed
into another state, also New, while some
stayed put, and so the old new became
a place to drive to, the tiny house near
the harbor, a stroll to stacked containers
and the loading docks of the refinery,
huge cranes lit up at night like Tivoli.

Development

I take a long-cut through the woods
to avoid the street my house is on.
Nothing is bound to happen:
the suburbs are safe enough,

but not the street my house is on.
I have a friend who lives nearby.
The suburbs are safe enough,
but the city is another story,

says my friend who lives nearby.
Her father came from Brooklyn,
where the city told another story.
Most of the parents come from there:

our mothers and fathers from Brooklyn,
Queens, the Bronx, and even Yonkers.
Most of them came from there.
They get along and ignore each other.

From Queens, the Bronx, and even Yonkers
came the Jews, the Irish, and the Italians,
who get along, or ignore each other.
The Serbo-Croatians, the Greeks,

the Jews, the Irish, and the Italians
of the United States of America,
the Serbo-Croatians and the Greeks,
all live on the same white streets

in the United States of America,
in old villages with small-town values.
Their kids, who live on the streets,
learn how to torture each other

with the tyranny of small-town values.
On our street of painted houses,
where we like to torture each other
with all of our differences

(as different as our painted houses),
I am smart, but he is stronger.
We name our differences
like enemies, but we are friends.

He's strong, but not so smart.
I grab him around the neck
like an enemy (though we are friends)
after he calls me what I am.

His sister grabs me around the neck
when I try to strangle him
for calling me what I am.
Anyway, I would have lost.

Or else I might have strangled him.
Instead, I yield to his confusion.
Years later, he gets lost
beside the river of change

in the forest of confusion.
Stumbling through the woods,
he follows that river
to the place where nothing happens.

Hat Trick

The child never came,
but the hats multiplied,
tissue-nested inside paper
drums, occasionally freed

to march in the parade
of Christmases and Easters.
Boxed during crises
and between church events,

they defined spaces inside
spaces. And as the Cape
cracked and moldered down
into the riverbed, hats

drifted up into corners:
cunning velvet placentas
stuck with matching pins,
straw hives and lace veils

sewn to bow and comb.
Crossed with one pheasant
feather, the high-crowned felt,
at attention in the dark,

shook discreetly at meetings.
The berets came out in winter
like fluffy flounders, took turns
being swallowed by the late

-model cetacean-blue Chevy—
a fedora with a tank, their first
and only automatic. Empty at last,
the house floated like a hat.

The Cherries of Kenwood

Gaze down these pink
tunnels into deeper pink.

The walls are blossoms
fashioned of smaller blossoms

attached to raised arms
that nuzzle other arms.

It's like watching a parade
that poses while I parade.

Random sprays liven up
the trunks, remind me to look up

at where naked limbs used to be.
Where the road used to be:

melted ice cream. A girl pedals
through a puddle of petals.

Little Kimono from Okinawa

For my first Halloween
as a white Jewish girl,
I was dressed in pink
silk flowers and an obi.
Something about a war.
Hobo, gypsy, trick
or treat for UNICEF.
We splayed our bags.
Years smeared beards
on patch-eyed pirates.
A rouged pallor lit
all the scary clowns
and one Southern belle,
whose mother sewed
her gown from scratch,
securing wire hoops
inside concentric tiers.
The witch phase passed
after spells were cast
and my breasts appeared.
Then nights were ghosts,
genderless, in sheets
and white by definition.
Pride would arrive later,
holding on to Shame.
Shaving cream and egg
mucous, arrhythmic thuds

of lobbed orange heads
kept the officers speeding
past the haunted houses
of razor blades and poison.
One foyer was famous
for a spread of naked fried
donuts. But that first time,
all I wanted was the candy,
a hand to hold, and not
to trip, or unwrap, or lose
the child I intended to be,
underneath, forever.

Flip Side

Vera lapped it up.
A pale mare with
a coyote ex, two wobbly

kids, our sweet boss
her bedroom secret.
Daddy Longlegs. I loved

him too. We parlayed
circle trays of swaying
glasses into quarters, neighed

in aqua houndstooth until
we all turned orange, molting
at the invisible order

from headquarters. Training
was on the house: shared
tips, no tip in that. From

her, I learned the ropes,
tossing monkey dishes
of syrup and creamer

at the regular brood
of truckers and troopers.
Men without women

perched at the counter
for the view. Dropped
change and flew.

I'm Painting the Little Bathroom

It has no sink. It's like a closet
with a window and a toilet

around which grew a thicket of paint cans,
aging wine, décor magazines,

and catalogs announcing expired sales.
You can't avoid the walls,

which look like veined retinas
where the paint has

separated. I scrape each groove out with a nail
and wipe it with a fingerful

of spackle. Then sand it smooth enough
to hide behind a layer of White Dove.

Finally, I apply the viscous skin
that holds the outside in.

Welcome to my bright little space
where I have hung a mirror for a face.

What is produced here
will mostly disappear,

and yet it is with some satisfaction that
I survey my work of white on white

as if it were a painting
by Ryman or Reinhardt, squinting

at the continuity of wall and ceiling
from which the light keeps falling,

a shade composed of red and green
and other colors that aren't seen,

and a diagram that lives inside of me,
if upside down and backward, actually.

Taken

I hate and I love.
    —Catullus

I was young. I wasn't afraid.
I was in love with poetry,
and he just wanted to get laid.

He waged a bet. I weighed
the odds. His take would be
me. A long shot. Unafraid,

I bet to win, and then I paid
with something he called destiny
because he wanted to get laid.

You wonder why I played,
knowing the game. Fuck me:
I should have been afraid.

The island was remote. I stayed
a week, waiting for the ferry. He
was a deity, so he got laid,

and I got rage to trade
for nausea when I left by sea
with hate, not love, afraid
of me. And he got laid.

Wire Artist

He bends them into the poses like wire,
then bends them out of wire.
The models are women for hire.

I read this in the paper
made of light. Then again in the paper
made of paper.

She claims he pulled her by the hair
and stuck his fingers into her.
Already there are twelve versions of her.

This man is not the artist.
He is an alleged rapist
who shares the front page with an artist.

The point is the women are the middlemen.
The point is he sells to rich men
who collect wire renderings of their hired women

as abstract sculpture so their wives won't know.
Probably their wives know.
Exaggerated sex parts show

through this hokey notion of abstraction.
Like money, it's not really an abstraction.
The rapist may face incarceration

if any of the allegations
become convictions. Convictions
generate more transactions.

The hired women get a cut.
The artist gets a cut.
The john gets a piece of wire art and a cunt,

and the college women testify in court.
Photography is banned there, so the court
artist turns them into art.

Fittings

How pomp surpassing ermine
When simple You, and I,
Present our meek escutcheon
and claim the rank to die!
—Emily Dickinson

A flange was similar to an escutcheon
except the flange was more of a pipe
with a flared rim, while the escutcheon
was a flat piece, a donut shape
that spanned the gap around the pipe
where the pipe entered the wall.
Flange also meant an undesirable
vagina (slang) while escutcheon
signified the pubic swatch in medicine,
as well as a shield in heraldry and
a ship's nameplate. Vessel and engine
were she, decked out in parts, as was the land
they sailed for. Also, Luck and Fortune,
and all the whales. The sea, but not the ocean.

Parts of the Chandelier

Each pendalogue is like a tear.
Five arms perform one duty
with an archaic beauty.

To make this clear,
I'd have to wipe the dust
from inside each bobèche fleur.

Form dictates five.
Their pistil wicks burn
without dripping wax

or consuming air.
One crystal sphere
sparked with sapphire

dangles from the axis:
the "bottom ball"
once coveted by children.

I can see us in the candle-
light that fell on snow
for hair, and glittering glasses:

the brilliant generations
circle around a center
that only they remember

and I forget to clean.
When girls turn cartwheels overhead,
the fixture rattles like a skeleton.

Terroir

Half of me came here
during Puccini's reign
from a place whose name
looks like a larder shelf

ending with a jar of jelly—
a lush green town
terraced with vineyards.
Somehow they sensed

in spite of this beauty
what was to come, or
maybe they didn't, exactly.
Call it fortune, or fear;

they had enough money
from their permitted work
(a distillery) for an idea:
here. Here needed more

brains and bodies, with
clothes to sew, bread
to bake, liquor to sell,
and restaurants to run

as my father's father did
with his brother. Long ago
departed, why did they come?
Letters in cramped script

beckoned. Citizenship
would be allowed, perhaps.
There was a Constitution:
laws and freedom both.

English was manageable
compared to their languages,
all the tongues in which
the revolution had failed.

English would marry them.
Mosaic cobblestone roads,
vineyards ruffled by wind—
each perfect harvest day

was assigned to a new owner
as circles were drawn
around the ones who stayed
to be picked, shipped, and slaughtered

with home still inside them.
My distillers were already here,
home fading inside them
as it turned into the earth

they walked on and the word
I taste—the must, the legs.
I practice it, now that I know
the name: Sátoraljaújhely.

Progression

Between two wars,
somebody snapped this picture
of a man poling past *Hardware*
in a hand-built dinghy.
The river found itself. *Tavern*
became *Inn*. Ritually fined
and padlocked, it was reborn
to limp along beside the tracks.
Soon three highways pierced
the town, a sign of weakness.
Then the train was gone.
Years later bulldozers came
to dredge the river that
we couldn't see through,
even when we crouched
next to it with paper cups.
A cement canyon opened
behind the new saloon.
Old regulars lined the bar,
waiting for the train to move.
The war was declared over,
like something you could measure.

Audiology

A simple excavation to remove
the occluding beaver dams of wax and hair
takes hours. A recalibrated pair
of crickets chirp, their chips in love

with a signal. The team positions them
in his flume's gloom, one in each ear.
So much to listen to, it's hard to hear.
Returning salmon undulate upstream,

the brightness focused by bionic lenses.
This is his last vacation of the senses;
the trip may be too loud, too colorful,
I'm told—a surreal edge to continuity.
Although I can see and hear perfectly,
my brain can barely fathom him at all.

(their new home)

My brain can barely fathom him at all.
After the usual hug, he fades away.
But when I wake him he wants me to stay
so I do. He perks up in the dining hall,

among familiar faces at the shared table.
The food's not bad. It's a Community.
Some still work, drive, head for the city.
Others are swallowed by the lower level,

but temporarily, the rest can hope.
Upstairs, absence is noted. Subdued chagrin
drops like a fork. You have to leave it there.
Waffles are eaten by the ones who dare.
The brains converse while spooning it all in.
Most would prefer to die in their sleep.

Most would prefer to die in their sleep,
not on the stage like tragic characters
whose deaths are written actions to rehearse
along with duels and kisses. Others stop

for death and give it lines to say.
Having survived another fall,
they reenter for the curtain call
to die and die again, day after day,

until life intervenes with quiet carnage.
The show goes on, but this old play is done,
at least for us. Our lead man has been cut.
He still has lines, but only speaks to one
at a time. A voice: my father is that.
For a while everything feels like a stage.

(his death)

For a while everything feels like a stage:
a prism of quietness to penetrate
with the machinery of set and plot
and the iconic inadequacies of language.

The end is written first. The imagination
wanders as far away as possible
not to surprise us, but to make us real.
Every sea is actually an ocean

and all the oceans are just one big one.
Time is the act of passing over it
from one wave to another. His was mine.
Jewish law provides one year to mourn
my wave. I measure it to make it fit.
I've been waiting all my life for this to happen.

(formalities)

I was waiting all my life for this to happen.
The days continue, oddly free of fear.
The weeks pass, ominously similar.
"A long life!" was comfort from a cousin,

her own loss unspeakable. Expressed sympathy
envelops the unsaid: condolences
sometimes reveal subliminal messages.
The formal ones are safest. They should be

(I was told) handwritten on good paper.
No verse is necessary; no purchased words
can outdo your own, in ink. A phone call
may stand in for a note (at least, an email).
He died in his sleep, I write, reread the cards
that say the same thing, over and over.

(his widow)

She says the same thing over and over.
She's an oracle in her own way, I guess.
The prophecy is her own loneliness
reflected in our faces when we answer.

Between each repetition is a space
for every parent bound to be a child
and every child wanting to be held.
Assumed connections between name and face

are absent, but the narrative holds fast;
it straps me in and takes me for a ride.
She is my mother, so I have to go with her,
but it's clear I never wanted to, inside.
He was the hunter, she the gatherer.
Her drawers are stuffed with coupons from the past.

(directions)

Her drawers are stuffed with coupons from the past
like tickets to a show no one remembers
except her. It had some lively numbers
and clever lyrics. The writer enters last

in a house coat, with china, silver, and a stain
remover. All of the coupons are expired,
but still redeemable if you're retired,
she assures me. There are spots in the brain

that come and go; some stay. "Take care of her":
he only said it once that I could hear.
He must have known she wasn't always there.
By then he was all echoing interior,
voice lost to need unheard. "Why did you hide
his hearing aids?" "They'll just get lost," she said.

(his mother)

Coda

She gave me Black Jack. *Licorice*, I said.
A nice young man with rosy cheeks, she sang.
A handsome sailor. I forget that song,
but not the gum. Soon she'll be dead,

but I don't understand. She was
herself, except she lost my name.
I go to look for it the way I came:
where the late day snags on shade trees

and tangle, by my boulder cave's secret
opening. Edging the path, ferns I love
harbor a sanctuary for toads. Parents
are not allowed, but childhood is, and it,
like any loss, explains itself by absence
no simple excavation will remove.

Children Sleeping

Snow on the mountain path
and the pines sweeping:
such a fresh breeze this June
morning and pillows cool.

I found this world
while you were sleeping
but you sleep on and on
as if you were the world.

You slept right through the bear
who shook the feeder.
You slept through rain
and waves of mist rising.

Where were you when
the river swelled its banks
and foamed up in curls
between the rocks?

Dreaming, with the water
pulled up to your necks,
while a downy woodpecker
hammered our day together.

Losing Words

Why doesn't it fall, hung
from the bottom up? *Cantilevered*

may be the word for this
bird. The plane tree

is not a plain tree.
A tweedy back disappears

into bark. The white
fleck, bulleted in red,

flickers. Nouns keep eating the verbs,
motion drawn into stillness

that precedes a blank
explosion. Then

the nouns go too.
No name for snow.

Buon Natale

The paper's rag nap holds
the hardness and the weight

of the woodblock, a cratered
version of the Befana reversed

in burnt sienna, her back almost
horizontal beneath the stuffed sack

of gifts. A fox curled around a tree.
Against mud and water, the creases

of her dress. The river doesn't carry
the geese, but makes way for them:

planted crookedly in the waves,
they look plump enough to hold.

A child might say they had no legs,
reading invisibility as absence.

The old December scene repeats itself
beyond pressure or relief, but how

my friend, the artist, inked the block
makes each card slightly different.

Before she died, I returned a few
per via aerea, words folded inside.

Horses

One life ends in a room
from which he could see
a red barn, black horses,

a river. Another life goes
on, the mind's harness
loosening, horses gone.

Double-Parked, with *Tosca*

I wonder if my neighbor with his dog
can hear "E lucevan le stelle"
exploding on the sidewalk
even though it's winter
and my glass is powered shut.
Someone is leaving;
someone waits for the space.
Every minute is a rat race.
Every evening is a rat fest.
The rats chew out the wires
from the bellies of the cars.
Our poison makes them tipsy.
They bleed to death inside.
They eat their young.
According to the announcer,
we are in act 3, the final act.
Mario the artist
loves Tosca the singer
and she loves him back.
A powerful psychopath
will destroy their future.
Mario will be shot
and Tosca will jump.
That will be that.
When art and love turn bad
for the powerless, and evil wins,

then it is time to sing.
Everyone is done.
Everyone is clapping.
My glass is empty of Puccini.
I toast him anyway,
hoot softly for the stars
as my blinkers flash
red on a small mountain of trash
recently sprinkled with dog urine
beneath which the rats keep singing.

Fitting Room

An edificial extraction not yet filled
with a taller form of the former normal
has unveiled a recessed battlement

whose curtains billow out and blinds
are caught at random angles with
the temporary shock of a horizon.

The new view from an old bedroom
freed from a quadrangle of bedrooms
must startle: an assumption

reborn as light on shuttered eyes,
a miracle as clear as clouds and sky,
the overlap of trees below skyscrapers,

and the moss-rimmed meer of surprise
into which a boy is dropping a line
one summer afternoon in July—

July 3rd to be exact—as traffic sews
and resews the seam of 110th Street
east and west. Take what you can

get, sleepyhead, now that it's given
—a glimpse of your own garden—
and know that it will be taken

by another sort of green. Soon
space will grow skin: walls, doors,
and mirrors. A life adjusts to the room

allotted. Inside an infinite retreat of light,
tenancy changes, shades of existence
and absence inevitably altering the view.

Intersection

Yellow's missing where
she built a nest, stuffed
that flashy snowman's
belly with insulation

that dribbles out between
red and green, eggs warmed
by a periodic pulse of gold
to which she returns

with a bird skip, workload
presumably lightened.
Tucked between go and stop
above the stop and go,

yolk-drunk heads emerge.
Wings unfold as traffic oozes
like a worm through dirt.
Announced by hay confetti,

knobby newborns descend
in slow spirals to the street.
Here we must leave them
in the hands of the drivers.

Heat

There is a look a bull gets
test-tasting a cow's urine

to see if she's fertile,
a kind of sneer or smile

(a curled lip means yes)
and when a ewe is truly

seeded, her tail sticks out
straight for hours, days

even. Just being mounted
can trigger heat, meaning

fertility, if not desire.
The hens don't need

a male, they still lay,
don't seem to miss

the rooster's dance, his
feet combing their backs,

his modest nub that's good
for the whole flock

to glom on to. Domestic
tom turkeys are too fat

for sex, but the females
still produce, knocked up

by humans with sperm-
filled turkey basters.

Unshorn sheep butt
and mount each other,

ewe to ewe like two
positives, head to head,

and now one is riding
another one's back like

what we made toys do.
The grass is getting

ready for them,
the days are brisk

and sunny, usually above
freezing, although

yesterday was snow.
By afternoon

they feel the heat
and lie down

like sweaty clouds
on melting clouds.

Algae

A pond dies of too much life.
Of warmth, of light.
What shouldn't kill it

does. Reflected trees
root and bloom; once real
they can't just come and go.

Our arms and faces ride
the slime forest, its food
our effluence, our past.

We would prefer a world without us
to dip our bodies in.

The Ice Pond

Still alive,
the pond freezes
and melts, can't decide.

It remembers
the stream that fills it
underground.

Caught in a circle
of hewn stone,
it shivers.

It wants what it wants.
But the mind
knows what it wants:

a house full of ice.
A warm house.

River Lesson

Lights replaced the lighthouse years ago.
The lighthouse keeper was eliminated,

his cottage modernized and filled with facts.
The facts, multiplying, will outlive the whales

for reasons that have yet to be confirmed.
A handful of the six or seven hundred

left to migrate through this region
have raised their backs into the rain

as if acknowledging the observation deck
constructed in their honor. A few white

backs breach the water. You can see
the young ones just below the surface.

They break and dive in unison, a dance
upstream, to where the shallows lift the food.

The milk of a lactating beluga female
has been deemed unfit for human consumption

due to the concentration of contaminants,
we read. Cadmium, aluminum, lead,

silver, mercury, titanium. The river is
blue and clear, the numbing cold invisible.

Fun

Speed makes him lighter   than the water

or maybe it's the gasoline   he's breathing in.

He wants to appear free   of where he's headed, turns away

from the relentless pressure forward   toward

us, and slices   the wake's ribbon into pieces.

Riding backward with no hands   he stands

briefly on the lake's skin   until the pixels fill him in.

Greeting

She sailed into the harbor
with her flag of hair
rivaling the brighter flags
on the data-driven yacht.

She stood on the deck
with the power of a girl
as Liberty's huge green
pose and poem passed

behind her. Mannahatta's
glass forest welcomed her
to its lowest, flattest part
where the salt tides rise

and fall, swell and rise.
Change is what we know,
said the child to the wind.
And the wind gave her to us.

Uses of Space

If the sculpture were human,
it would feel ignored

by the receptionist.
She doesn't choose which way she's facing.
The chair does. But someone chose the chair,
positioned it to face the door.
Someone else chose the sculpture

and made it stand beside her.
The room seems too large
and the woman too small,
but the sculpture seems important.

It's a large fan of scrap metal
like a helicopter
that's been written on
and spray-painted.

No, it's a windmill. Body heat
would turn the turbines,
said the artist in an interview.

The artist
is famous. The artist
is dead. In his lifetime he came to understand
economics. Some
don't like this art
or consider it necessary.

This room is large enough for a small
wedding reception.

The receptionist is jealous
of the sculpture,
which has managed to secrete
all its money in a tax haven
offshore, safe
from the divorce settlement.
The sculpture is rich
and she is in debt.
They don't speak.

Or else she loves the sculpture.
Sometimes she is a man.
The sculpture can be either sex
or both: it has stiff
appendages, one big tit.

In any case, they are both in the same business.

In this city, where homeless people sleep against
cold glass cubes of vacant space,
such habitats were cultivated for the vetted guest,
with a view of life from afar, an abstract panorama
of ourselves as spires, bridges, and rivers,
below which the carpet was the palest green,
as if conceived from the impossible
marriage of dune to ocean.

The windmill's sails are sharp.
I am done here. Power,
blow me a kiss.

Salt and Fresh

During the hurricane, sea
wandered through the aquarium,

her wide shoulders against
the glass. Suddenly, some

tenants felt lighter. The koi
expired, but the sharks

breathed deeper. Horses
pedaled in redundant pockets.

Skates and angels rose toward heaven.
Outside, trees were confused

at the root. In one living
room, sea blanketed a parrot

cage on which a live
pit bull was balanced.

Light Metal

Pastel confections in the sky
that make us like the dark
are empty offices by day
where people used to work.

The pink spire of Times Square,
the chameleon Empire State,
our twisted Freedom Tower
that always glitters white

compete with newer renderings
outlined in red or blue
to alert low-flying things
as they reinvent the view,

if only for themselves.
But they can't see themselves.

Moving Poem

It's a box like all the other boxes, but
everything fits, and nothing stays behind.
Nothing fits and everything stays behind,
I mean. Either way, it starts out flat,

like a piece of land, with corrugations
of terrain, and mountains in the clouds,
and rays of light penetrating the clouds
over war, pestilence, and migrations—

suffering and suffering avoided.
There are instructions printed on the box
and even if I stand outside the box,
I still end up inside the flaps I folded,

labeled by luck, or someone else's fear.
I'll be looking at this box until I die.
I was delivered once, and when I die,
I'll also be delivered. Track me here.

The Garden

He is the pear before the leaf,
flower before the seed is sown.
She is the tear before the grief,
but he is the pear before the leaf.

She is the loss before the thief.
She is of him, but still her own.
He is the wreck before the reef.
She is the flesh before the stone.

She is the pear before the leaf,
harvest before the seed is sown.
He is the tear before the grief,
and she is the fall before the leaf.

She is the grain before the sheaf.
She is like him, but still her own.
He is the blight before the reef.
She is the grave before the bone.

Intrepid

The wall of my gray hold
is a tsunami in dry dock,
one perfect heft frozen
above landlocked motion
of foot and wheel. But

above that I'm a doormat,
a plateau, a landing strip
for marvels and electorates.
Call me Latin for what I'm not:
afraid. I contain all fear

in my metal's mettle, I hold
myself so tight you can't look
up my skirt. My toes curl
seven decks below, my lashes
are pinioned on a tower and

there's lace around my deck.
On my chest, the old moon
shuttle Discovery perches
like an aphid on a rose leaf.
The sun breaches Queens

and bails out in Bayonne,
but I never shade my eyes.
I take the heat all day,
but in cool night, I give it up.
I'm awesome and I'm tragic:

I used to be in the theater.
I have a center that burns oil,
an island that's my brain,
and I carry two kinds of fuel—
one for me and one to leave me.

No matter how many fill me,
I'm still a vessel. Hollow
is my definition. Hallowed
be my name. Abandoned
is my duty. Salute me.

Tick Tock

How calmly, host,
you yield, so unaware
that you were taken
and that you took.

Numbing your skin,
I tendered easily
with one sharp shove
my little parcel.

I'll end our kiss
with my extraction
—one drop of blood—
and your contraction:

cold hands, warm belly,
neck as stiff as oak,
the fear of future ache,
stroke, madness, death.

And then I'll wait
—for I don't have to eat—
on this damp blade
for any passing fancy.

Creative Writing

My son shows me a poem
about fishing with his father

as imagined by the fish.
How it feels to be held

when you have no hands,
to freeze as a question mark

is slipped from your numb lip.
Gripping the rod (he writes)

is a small hand
inside a larger hand.

Beneath the green confusion
of the trees, one thing holds

another. The father releases
the trout. The towers go down.

He was told to rewrite the end—
so far from the beginning.

But even so, I understand
the arbitrary nature of endings.

I liked his poem.
It was all I could do.

Singing to Water

I'm falling, sings the water.
Here's my version, sings the bird.

I'm leaving, sings the water.
I hear you, sings the bird.

They sing in tandem, not together.
Neither understands the other

nor does it matter.
It's a sound marriage.

Someone turns on the faucet.
Someone sweeps up the feathers.

The water sings the song
of what it touches.

The bird sings because
the water does.

As plumage distills light,
the water holds it

in one silver thread
like a plucked string.

Sharps and flats escape
from rattled bars and frets.

I'm flying, sings the water.
I'm flying, sings the bird.

The Letter *S*

A spine is where the water used to be,
and around it, the hard organ
rocks in disarray. Once it was a snake
glistening a path through the rough bank
with curvatures, a slow turning
in place, but now it's just a place
holder, noting the preferred way down,
if down should again prove necessary,
past signatures of moss and clover.
Where past and future used to swim
is a sloughed skin pressed between
the pages of my dictionary, pinned
to its entry by the weight of layered
moth wings, beside a penciled date.

Divine Peacock

He does the April strut
in Busby Berkeley white
and fascinator hat.
Tumescence floats his skirt

like Marilyn's, in thrall
to waves of cherry tulle
beside the implacable
stones of the cathedral.

To have lived this long
and still feel young
is a fashionable thing.
You hum the old song;

I wear the vintage dress.
We know what some can't guess.
Gorgeous, tremble with us
against the lit surfaces.

Orchestra as Landscape

At the flute's
horizon,
twin cymbal suns
reflect cello rain

that bows the trees
and silences
the violin bees.
Thunder comes

when summoned.
The harp rainbow
fingers promise
as the piccolo

bird, our most
American piper,
sails up to roost
in the fall gold

of the brass:
French, English,
and spreading tuba.
The soloist is

skirted in sky
at the piano's lake.
Power lines hum.
Reeds break.

Our Egret

A dogged flight path, sagging with the weight
of congealed marshes, smoke, a derailed train

stuck in the Meadowlands, anticipated freight
spread out like rubble in the mud and rain,

removes her to the calm of Central Park,
where, settling into place at the north end,

wading almost unseen in the half-dark,
she plucks a minnow from the stocked pond,

and, steadying herself with a small lift of wings,
funnels it down, inside concentric rings.

Heavy Metal

You take the music, but I'll keep the names:
dead cardinal doused in flames,

old magpie clown,
and when this racket's nearly done,

the indigo bunting's set
between blue and violet.

Kestrel, grackle, titmouse, tanager.
Kingbird. Good nightjar.

Reverse Farm

On the far side of the island
where the trees waded knee-deep,

switchgrass doubled itself in water.
That was where the herons bred

in enforced privacy. But on
the near side, above a ledge of rock,

a field broke free and sun poured in.
Blooming onions pierced a rusted wheel

laid flat to steer; drunken hops
collapsed on spent walls. Orphan

hay was tangled up with loosestrife
and it felt like we were dancing—

at least as I remember it.
The arthritic orchard, churchlike

behind the stunted pines,
held on to its old idea.

Around us tufted water drew
the only kind of line it wanted to

and because no one else was there
we lay down in the open.

Ellen Kaufman's first collection, *House Music*, was a finalist for the Able Muse Book Award (Able Muse, 2013). A poem from that book won the Morton Marr Poetry Prize awarded by *Southwest Review*, where it also appeared. Her poems have also been published by *Beloit Poetry Journal, Carolina Quarterly, Epoch, Hampden-Sydney Poetry Review*, the *New Yorker, Poetry Northwest, Salamander, Shenandoah*, the *Yale Review*, and other literary magazines. Twice a MacDowell Fellow (2009 and 2013), she holds an AB from Cornell, and MFA and MSLS degrees from Columbia University. Formerly a poetry reviewer for *Library Journal*, she now reviews for *Publishers Weekly*. She lives near Straus Park in upper Manhattan.

Richard Newman, *All the Wasted Beauty of the World — Poems*

Alfred Nicol, *Animal Psalms — Poems*

Deirdre O'Connor, *The Cupped Field (Able Muse Book Award for Poetry)*

Frank Osen, *Virtue, Big as Sin (Able Muse Book Award for Poetry)*

Alexander Pepple (Editor), *Able Muse Anthology;*
    Able Muse — A Review of Poetry, Prose & Art (semiannual, winter 2010 on)

James Pollock, *Sailing to Babylon — Poems*

Aaron Poochigian, *The Cosmic Purr — Poems;*
    Manhattanite (Able Muse Book Award for Poetry)

Tatiana Forero Puerta, *Cleaning the Ghost Room — Poems*

Jennifer Reeser, *Indigenous — Poems*

John Ridland, *Sir Gawain and the Green Knight (Anonymous) — Translation;*
    Pearl (Anonymous) — Translation

Stephen Scaer, *Pumpkin Chucking — Poems*

Hollis Seamon, *Corporeality — Stories*

Ed Shacklee, *The Blind Loon: A Bestiary*

Carrie Shipers, *Cause for Concern (Able Muse Book Award for Poetry)*

Matthew Buckley Smith, *Dirge for an Imaginary World*
    (Able Muse Book Award for Poetry)

Susan de Sola, *Frozen Charlotte — Poems*

Barbara Ellen Sorensen, *Compositions of the Dead Playing Flutes — Poems*

Rebecca Starks, *Time Is Always Now — Poems;*
    Fetch Muse — Poems

Sally Thomas, *Motherland — Poems*

J.C. Todd, *Beyond Repair — Poems*

Paulette Demers Turco (Editor), *The Powow River Poets Anthology II*

Rosemerry Wahtola Trommer, *Naked for Tea — Poems*

Wendy Videlock, *Slingshots and Love Plums — Poems;*
    The Dark Gnu and Other Poems;
    Nevertheless — Poems

Richard Wakefield, *A Vertical Mile — Poems;*
    Terminal Park — Poems

Gail White, *Asperity Street — Poems*

Chelsea Woodard, *Vellum — Poems*

Rob Wright, *Last Wishes — Poems*

www.ablemusepress.com

www.ingramcontent.com/pod-product-compliance
Lightning Source LLC
Chambersburg PA
CBHW031359060726
47590CB00007B/2855